Righteous Rockers

Bo DIDDLEY

Nicole K. Orr

PURPLE TOAD PUBLISHING

Printing 1 2 3 4 5 6 7 8 9

PUBLISHER'S NOTE
This series, Righteous Rockers, covers racism in United States history and how it affected musicians and others. Some of the events told in this series may be disturbing to young readers.

Bo Diddley
by Nicole K. Orr

Chuck Berry
by Wayne L. Wilson

Fats Domino
by Michael DeMocker

Little Richard
by Wayne L. Wilson

Sam Cooke
by Wayne L. Wilson

ABOUT THE AUTHOR: Nicole K. Orr has been writing for as long as she's known how to hold a pen. She is the author of several other titles by Purple Toad Publishing and has won National Novel Writing Month eleven times. Orr lives in Portland, Oregon, and camps under the stars whenever she can. When she isn't writing, she's traveling the world or taking road trips.

Library of Congress Cataloging-in-Publication Data
Orr, Nicole K.
Bo Diddley / Written by Nicole K. Orr
p. cm.
Includes bibliographic references, glossary, and index.
ISBN 9781624694066
1. Diddley, Bo, 1928-2008 — Juvenile literature. 2. Singer, guitarist, songwriter — United States — Biography — Juvenile literature. 3. African American Rock and Roll Musicians — Biography — Juvenile literature. I. Series: Righteous Rockers
ML420.A45 2019
787.87
[B]

Library of Congress Control Number: 2018943797
ebook ISBN: 9781624694059

Contents

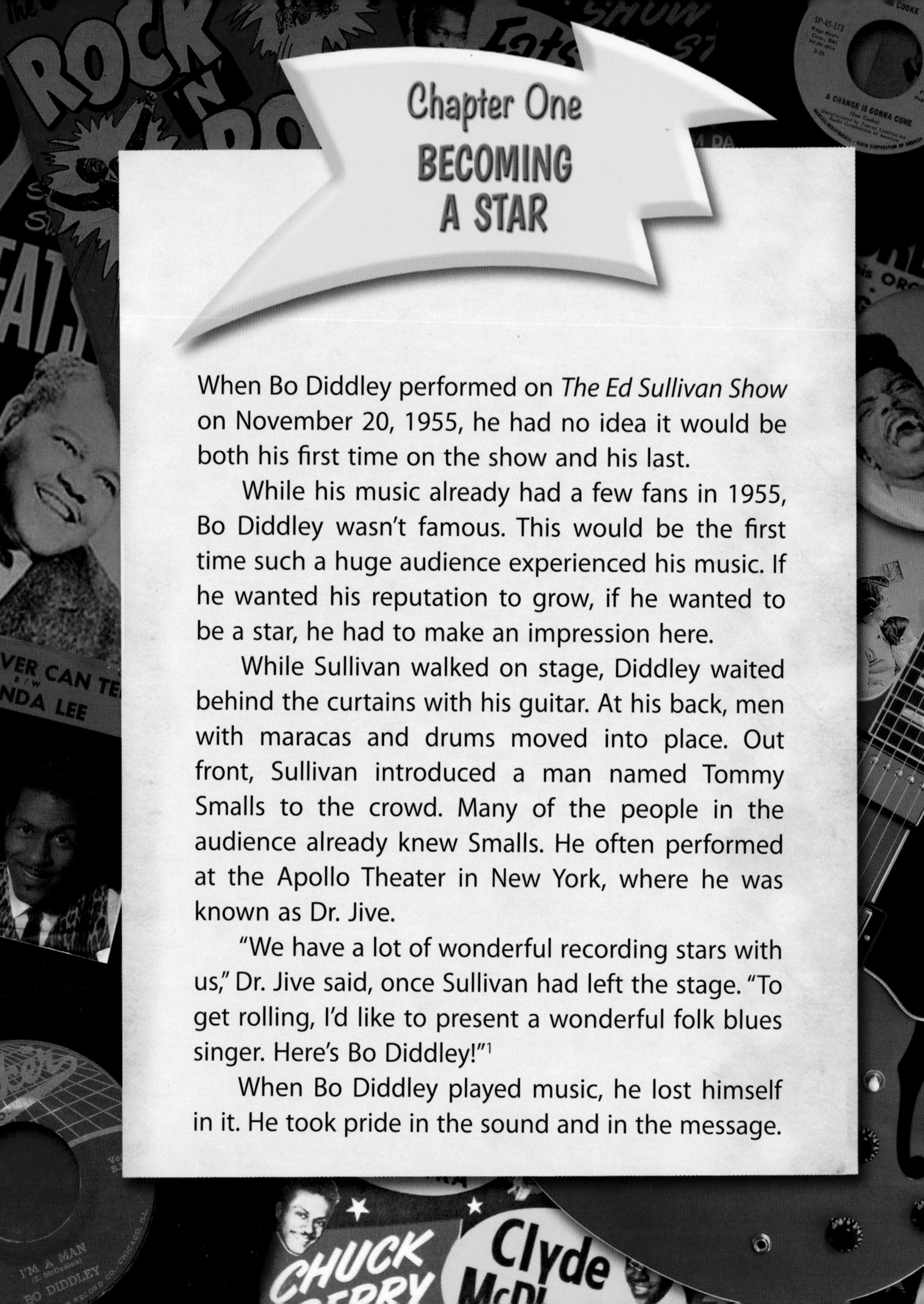

Chapter One
BECOMING A STAR

When Bo Diddley performed on *The Ed Sullivan Show* on November 20, 1955, he had no idea it would be both his first time on the show and his last.

While his music already had a few fans in 1955, Bo Diddley wasn't famous. This would be the first time such a huge audience experienced his music. If he wanted his reputation to grow, if he wanted to be a star, he had to make an impression here.

While Sullivan walked on stage, Diddley waited behind the curtains with his guitar. At his back, men with maracas and drums moved into place. Out front, Sullivan introduced a man named Tommy Smalls to the crowd. Many of the people in the audience already knew Smalls. He often performed at the Apollo Theater in New York, where he was known as Dr. Jive.

"We have a lot of wonderful recording stars with us," Dr. Jive said, once Sullivan had left the stage. "To get rolling, I'd like to present a wonderful folk blues singer. Here's Bo Diddley!"[1]

When Bo Diddley played music, he lost himself in it. He took pride in the sound and in the message.

The rectangular guitar he designed, trademark black-rimmed glasses, and lyrics that could make you laugh as much as dance: It must be Bo Diddley!

Tennessee Ernie Ford had a hit in "Sixteen Tons," but he also tried his hand at rock and roll with "Rock, Roll, Boogie" in 1956.

Tonight, he was supposed to play a song belonging to another musician named Tennessee Ernie Ford. The song was "Sixteen Tons," and Diddley had performed it before. Crowds loved that tune!

History would never quite be able to agree on just why Bo Diddley didn't play the song he was supposed to play. Did he not want to play something by a white person? Did he get confused and play the wrong song by accident? The most common theory is that Diddley did it on purpose. He knew this was his one chance to show his skills as a musician. He wanted people to remember his face, his skin, his music, and his message, not that of Tennessee Ernie Ford! With that in mind, Diddley changed his plans. He played the song titled "Bo Diddley."[2]

By the time Sullivan realized what Bo Diddley was doing, it was too late. Diddley was already on the stage and playing. All Sullivan could do was stand out of sight, watch the performance, and then order the curtains shut before Diddley could begin another song.

Diddley was confused and insulted when he went to talk to the host of the show. There was a lot of swearing and name-calling. Sullivan accused Diddley of betraying him. Diddley tried to explain that the song he'd named after himself was more important.

Ed Sullivan's show was known for welcoming African American performers—which was rare for the time.

The famous Ed Sullivan Theater marquee in New York City advertises the night the Beatles performed in 1964.

Today, the Ed Sullivan Theater is home to *The Late Show with Stephen Colbert*.

Sullivan, however, did not like surprises. He told the musician that not only was he banned from *The Ed Sullivan Show*, but Diddley would never be on another TV show for the rest of his life.[3]

Ed Sullivan managed to keep Diddley from ever stepping onto his stage again, but nobody could keep the blues singer from getting his music out into the world. In fact, his one appearance on *Sullivan* helped launch his career.

The Ed Sullivan Theater marquee in 2018. It still rests over Angelo's Pizza, which continues to serve food after all these years.

WHAT IS BLUES MUSIC?

Many forms of music borrow from the blues, but blues music is still very different from those other styles. In the beginning, the blues were not performed on stage or recorded for wide audiences. They were songs that slaves sang while working in the fields. As time passed, the songs changed. They were less songs and more spoken stories. These were what Bo Diddley would one day play.

Traditionally, the blues were associated almost entirely with the African American community. In 1908, a song was written by Antonio Maggio called "I Got the Blues." Most sources agree that this was the first published blues song.

Blues musician Willie Dixon described the blues this way: "The blues are the roots and the other musics are the fruits. It's better keeping the roots alive, because it means better fruits from now on. The blues are the fruits of all American music. As long as American music survives, so will the blues."[4] While Bo Diddley transformed the blues to rock and roll, it was Dixon's opinion that the blues inspired all genres of music that followed.

Willie Dixon wrote his first song when he was just 14 years old. Later, he also wrote screenplays.

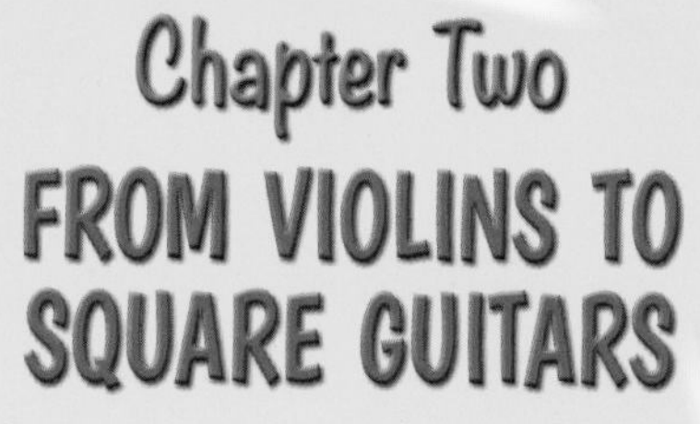

Chapter Two
FROM VIOLINS TO SQUARE GUITARS

Bo Diddley changed the world of blues music and of rock and roll. Because of the music he created—and how he inspired other musicians and bands—he became known as the Originator. Long before he was called that, of course, he went by another name.

Very little is known about Bo Diddley's childhood. He was born on December 30, 1928, in McComb, Mississippi. For the first few years of his life, he went by the name his mother had given him: Ellis Landry. (Some sources report it as *Elias*.) His mother was Ethel Wilson. Ethel, Ellis, and Ellis's half brother Kenneth were living with Eugene Bates, a cousin of Ethel's. Ellis thought of Eugene as a father, so he took his last name: Ellis Landry Bates. As an unmarried woman, Ethel never revealed the identity of Ellis's father.

Ellis was around eight years old when he was adopted by another cousin of his mother's, Gussie McDaniel. When this happened, he took her last name instead and became Ellis Landry McDaniel. By the late 1930s, Gussie McDaniel moved with him to

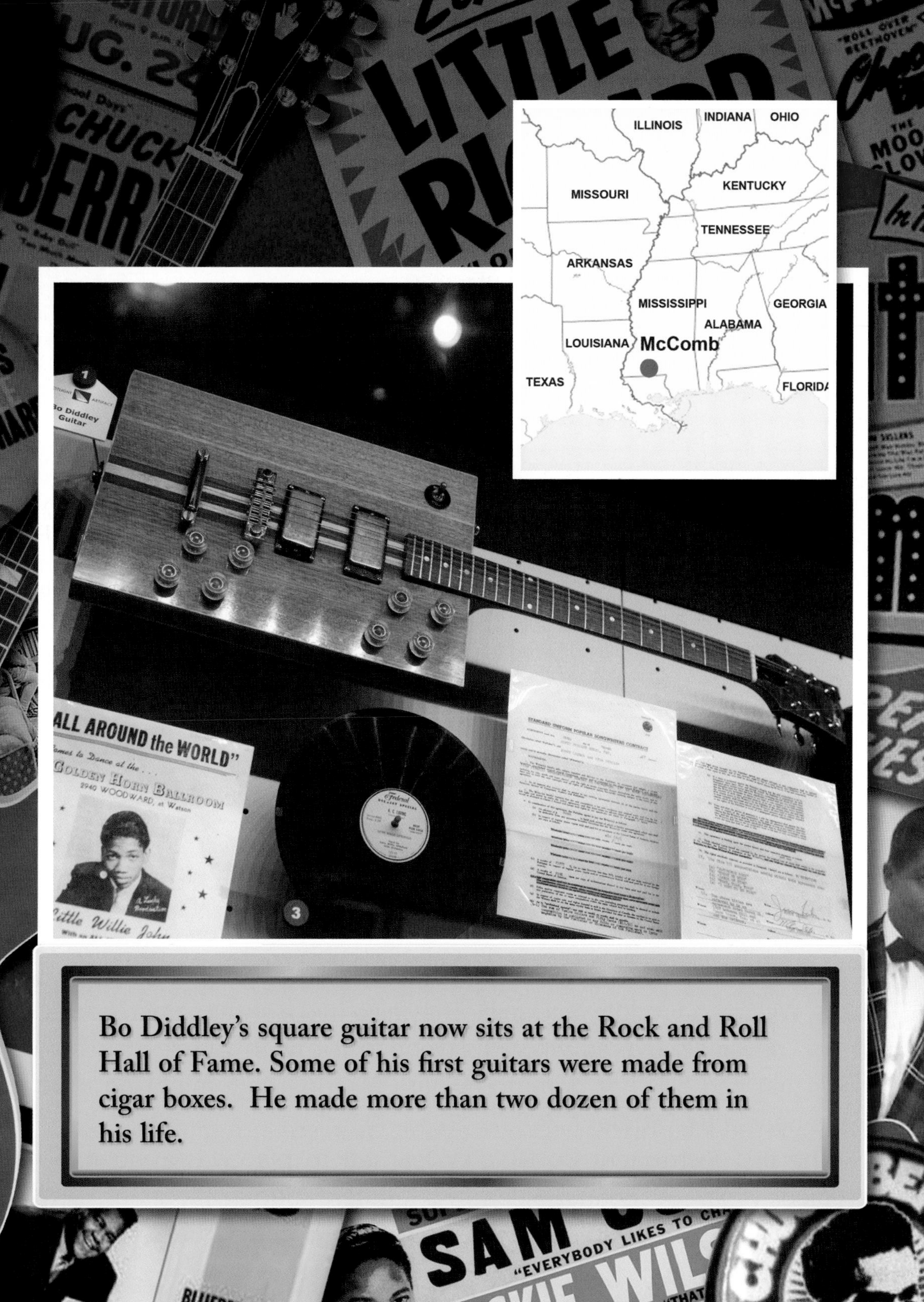

Bo Diddley's square guitar now sits at the Rock and Roll Hall of Fame. Some of his first guitars were made from cigar boxes. He made more than two dozen of them in his life.

Musicians often played on street corners in Chicago's South Side (above).

Chicago, Illinois. There, she raised him as a son with her other two boys, Willis and Freddie McDaniel. They also had a sister named Lucille. It was never discovered why Ellis went to live with Gussie. It is only clear that had Ellis not gone to live in Chicago, there might not ever have been a Bo Diddley.[1]

The first instrument Bo Diddley learned to play was a violin. He studied violin at Ebenezer Baptist Church, under Professor O.W. Frederick. After the violin, he grew fascinated with drums. It wasn't

John Lee Hooker became a music legend in his own right. His boogie sound became known as Hooker-style guitar.

until he was around 12 that a song on the radio changed everything. The music was by blues musician John Lee Hooker. After hearing that song, Bo decided he was done with the violin and drums. Sister Lucille gave him a guitar, and Bo was off![2]

When Bo was around 15 years old, he enrolled at the Foster Vocational High School in Chicago. There, he learned how to build his own musical instruments, including violins and guitars. He got creative with his designs, going as far as building a square guitar. "I just decided to make a square one and see if it worked, and it did, so I used it in my act."[3]

Bo couldn't wait to share his music with the world. Sometime in his teens, he began playing on street corners. He became a common sight on Chicago's Maxwell Street. As time passed, the tips got better and the crowds got bigger. Soon enough, Bo was playing in local clubs. In 1951, he met two other musicians—Jody Williams and Billy Boy Arnold. Diddley supposedly said to them, "We're going to the Midway Theater, right up the street, and do an amateur show. Come

It was not uncommon to see performers playing on Maxwell Street.

Street musicians entertain with an accordion and a washboard. The washboard was used to keep time in many musical forms.

on and go down there with me!"[4] Not long after this, the three musicians began playing on street corners together.

Bo Diddley, Billy Boy Arnold, and Jody Williams created a band that included a washboard and maracas, as well as Arnold's harmonica. The band was first named The Hipsters, but was later changed to The Langley Avenue Jive Cats. Together, the men's popularity grew. By 1954, they were performing regularly at bars in Chicago, like Sawdust Trail and Castle Rock. Since the three men wanted to find a record company to sell their music, they created a demo. They recorded a song or two and then made a lot of copies. They gave them out to as many record companies as they could.

Bo was building a name for himself fast, but not everybody in his life was happy for him. The church where he had first learned to love music was upset. They called his lyrics "the devil's music" because he wrote about topics the church did not approve of. When even Gussie McDaniel, Bo's adoptive mother, started agreeing with the church, he left home.

Bo Diddley's music had a life to it. He thought maybe he could live off that.

Rock and roll was often called "the devil's music" by people who didn't like it. Blues legend Robert Johnson played so well, it was said he sold his soul to the devil at a crossroads for success.

WHERE DID BO DIDLEY GET HIS NAME?

When it comes to Diddley's early life, there isn't much on which historians can agree. One mystery is where Diddley got his stage name. What is known is that he became Bo Diddley sometime after he moved to Chicago with Gussie McDaniel. Beyond that, there are numerous theories. Did Bo give himself the title or did someone else give it to him? Was Bo named after the one-stringed African guitar called a "diddley bow"? In the days of Bo's childhood, there was a comedian who sometimes performed at the Indiana Theater named Bo Diddley. Had Bo been named after him? Is it possible he got the title because of a singer his adoptive mother knew? One theory suggests the name came from the slang term *diddley squat*, which translates to "absolutely nothing." One of the main reasons that no one knows how the blues singer got his title is because the man himself told different stories each time he was asked. Besides the stories, Billy Boy Arnold offered yet another explanation—as nonsense lyrics.

Example of an electric diddley bow, complete with attached pickup for amplified sound and a bottle for a bridge

Chapter Three
DISCOVERING THE DIDDLEY BEAT

The same year Bo Diddley performed on *The Ed Sullivan Show*, he also found a record company interested in his blues music. It was 1955 and Diddley had just met Leonard Chess. Chess owned Chess Records, and he wanted Diddley and Billy Boy Arnold to write him one or two songs. The pressure was intense, but the reward was huge. It is controversial whether Diddley gave Chess two songs or one, but the most common theory is that he sent him two. The first was "I Am a Man." During this time period, African American men were often called "boy," no matter what their age. The lyrics of "I Am a Man" focused on the role of a man and sent a message: "I am not a boy. I am a man." The other tune was titled simply "Bo Diddley." Diddley used this to show off the new beat he loved and would later become famous for. It was sometimes referred to as doing the hambone. Diddley based it on the leg-slapping beat he remembered from church.

"I Am a Man" was very popular, but "Bo Diddley" made the artist famous.

The Bo Diddley beat went on to inspire other classic songs such as “Not Fade Away” by Buddy Holly and “Magic Bus” by The Who.

Billy Boy Arnold (above) grew up next door to blues legend Sonny Boy Williamson in Chicago. Williamson taught Billy how to play the harmonica, which Arnold played on many Bo Diddley records.

There are at least a dozen theories about why and how Bo Diddley got his name. Billy Boy Arnold added his story to the list. He told journalist Richie Unterberger that the name was invented during the writing of "Bo Diddley." "He was singing 'Papa gonna buy his babe a diamond ring' and playing the hambone beat. And I suggested, why don't you say, 'Bo Diddley'? That's how that name came into the picture." Arnold went on to say that when Chess Records released their first single, he and Diddley were surprised. Not only was the song titled "Bo Diddley," but the title of the artist was the same.[1]

When Diddley and Arnold were recording at Chess Studios, Leonard Chess routinely gave Diddley the most attention. Arnold realized very quickly that Chess didn't like him very much. "He told Bo he didn't like that harmonica player. Not the music, but my personality," Arnold said in the interview with Unterberger.[2] When Diddley suggested that Arnold find another company, Arnold agreed and began recording for Vee-Jay Records instead. Arnold still used the Diddley Beat, and his popularity grew very fast.

This leg-slapping, hand-clapping, foot-stomping routine had already made two men popular. What would it do next?

During the first part of Diddley's life, music was still largely segregated according to race. White people listened to music by white

Chess Studios represented many famous musicians besides Diddley. These included legends Muddy Waters, Chuck Berry, and Willie Dixon. Dixon was considered one of the main contributors to what was later called "The Chess Records Sound."

A crowd dances in a style that originated as a 1930s African American dance style. As early rock and roll caught on, people from all races began to dance to it.

musicians. Black people listened to music by black musicians. At the start, the blues were mostly enjoyed by African Americans. As time went by, however, blues music began to bridge the gap between races and be enjoyed by all.

By appealing to all races, his music was helping the civil rights movement. As writer Barbara Beebe said, "Long before civil rights marchers held signs saying, 'I AM A MAN,' Bo Diddley was singing about it."[3]

There was a message in Bo Diddley's music, but not everyone heard it. Believing this message was worth spreading as far as he could, Bo Diddley went on tour.

THE HAMBONE

The Diddley Beat has become very popular in blues music, but there was a time where it went by a different name: the hambone. In the days before the Civil War (1861–1865), slavery was common across the United States, especially in the South. Enslaved people were forced to work very hard. Men would spend their days in the fields under the hot sun. Women would spend their days either in the fields or doing laundry and cooking meals for their white owners.

By late evening, some slaves could finally relax and play music. However, most were forbidden to use drums. To get a beat going, they would slap their legs, clap their hands, or smack two sticks together. This percussion became known as the hambone.

After slavery ended, the hambone lived on in church songs and other African American music. Bo Diddley used that beat, as well as the hand jive, the Juba dance, and the children's game pat-a-cake, to create the Diddley Beat.

The Old Plantation **shows slaves dancing on a South Carolina plantation. It was probably painted between 1785 and 1790.**

Chapter Four
FROM COVER TO COVERED

Successes came faster and faster for Bo Diddley. He toured the United States and overseas. He performed in bars and in stadiums. He proved Ed Sullivan wrong and played his music on TV again. Often performing in a pair of sunglasses and a black hat, Diddley had perfected his own look too. His songs were getting more recognition as well. His first song, "Bo Diddley," did extremely well on the R&B charts. With each song he released, he gained more fans. In 1956, "Pretty Things" reached the top 40 in R&B. In 1962, "You Can't Judge a Book by Its Cover" hit number 21 on the R&B charts. Some of Diddley's other popular tunes were "Who Do You Love," "Mona," and "Before You Accuse Me."

As Diddley wrote more songs, he played alongside more musicians and bands. Some of these were Little Water, Willie Dixon, Earl Hooker, and Chuck Berry. He also played with musicians such as drummers Clifton James and Frank Kirkland, as well as piano player Otis Spann. There was also Lester Davenport with his harmonica, and Jerome Green, who handled the bass and maracas.

The band Red Cloud takes the stage before one of Diddley's gigs. Diddley like to give bands on the rise the chance to open for him and make a name for themselves.

The Rolling Stones recorded Bo Diddley's song *Mona*. They credit him with being an enormous influence in rock and roll history.

Chess Records continued to produce Diddley's albums—11 of them—between 1958 and 1963. The more songs Diddley created, the more bands and musicians did covers of them. These other artists would perform the same song but in a different style. Diddley was especially flattered when white bands began covering his blues. Among these were the rock bands the Rolling Stones, the Yardbirds, and Pretty Things. This last one had taken their name from Bo Diddley's song of the same title.

In 1964, Eric Burdon and The Animals wrote a song about him, called "The Story of Bo Diddley." It describes Diddley coming to their show to hear them play some of his tunes, and Diddley declares the music "the biggest load of rubbish I ever heard in my life."[1] Did this ever happen? As Eric Burdon told Bradley Mason Hamlin in 2009, he had invited Diddley to come to the show, but Diddley didn't show up. He was such a huge fan, though, he wanted to reach out to Diddley. When he wrote the song, Burdon says, "I was in the mindset, don't let the truth get into the way of a good story," and he told "how Bo Diddley did actually visit the club."[2]

Eric Burdon of The Animals greatly admired Bo Diddley. Besides their hit "House of the Rising Sun," The Animals also covered songs by Diddley, Chuck Berry, and John Lee Hooker.

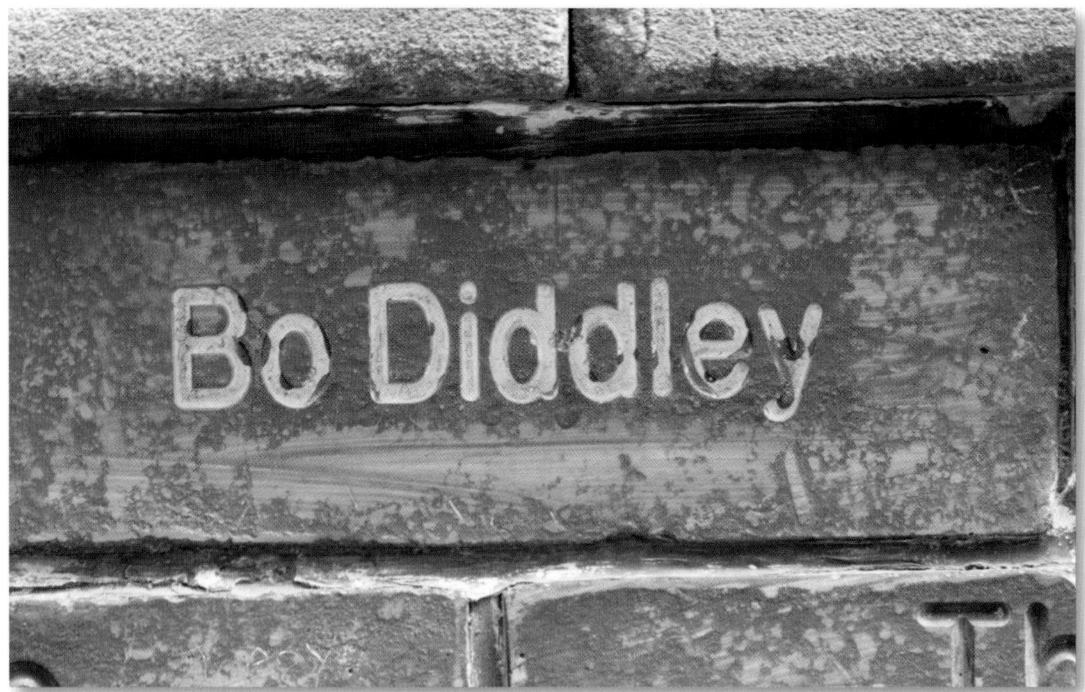

Bo Diddley's name is enshrined on the hall of fame wall at the famous Cavern Club in Liverpool, England. British groups all over London, England in the 1960s played Diddley's music, including the Beatles.

At one time, Diddley had to play on street corners in order to get an audience. Now, black and white people were buying his albums, and white bands were playing his tunes and singing about him.

Not everything in Diddley's life was going smoothly. He might have been a rising blues star, but it hadn't helped his personal life. He was married a total of four times, all of which ended in divorce. He had four children. Despite his fame, Diddley had always had trouble with money because record companies were not paying him much for his work. Throughout his career, he'd had to work jobs on the side, including as a boxer, carpenter, and mechanic. At one point, he sold the rights to some of his songs so that he could pay for the education of his kids.

These money problems might be one of the reasons that, in 1971, Diddley moved to Los Lunas, New Mexico. There, he played two roles.

He kept producing his music, and he served as the city's deputy sheriff for over two years.

Diddley received a lot of invitations to open for other bands or partner with them on performances. He played with a great variety of musicians, including the Clash, the Everly Brothers, Little Richard, Alan Freed, and the Grateful Dead. In 1973, Diddley was in the music documentary *Let the Good Times Roll* along with other musicians, including Chuck Berry. In 1976, the Radio Corporation of America (RCA) released the music album *The 20th Anniversary of Rock 'n' Roll* in honor of Diddley.

The Grateful Dead played a set with Diddley on March 25, 1972. They were such big fans, they went on to play Diddley songs many times. Mickey Hart, the drummer for the band, said this after Diddley's death: "Rock the heavens, Mr. Diddley, like only you can."[3]

While his health slowed him down later in life, Diddley's work kept him moving.

Diddley was also briefly in the movie industry. He played a pawnbroker in the 1983 film *Trading Places*. Then, in 1998, he was in *Blues Brothers 2000*.

In the early 1980s, Diddley met Faith Fusillo, who became his business manager. She also started a company called Talent Source, which would grow to represent just Bo Diddley.

Meanwhile, in 1989, advertisers for Nike sportswear asked him to appear in an advertising campaign called "Bo Knows." Nike was selling a new line of cross-trainers, shoes for athletes who play more than one sport. Bo Jackson, who played both baseball and football, was in all of the ads in the campaign. He is shown with professionals from many different sports. When he is shown with baseball player Kirk Gibson, Gibson says, "Bo knows baseball." When he is shown with football player Jim Everett, Everett says, "Bo knows football." The ads continue showing Jackson with star athletes from various other sports. One of the ads in the series features music by Bo Diddley. It starts the same way as the other ads, but then it shows Bo Jackson trying to learn guitar from Bo Diddley. It does not go well for Jackson. The scene

Bo Jackson is considered one of the greatest athletes in history. In his baseball career, he hit 141 home runs in 694 games.

Diddley continued to play on homemade square guitars throughout his life.

ends with Diddley telling Jackson, "Bo, you don't know Diddley!" For a while, it was common to hear people say, "Bo, you don't know Diddley" to someone who didn't know how to do something.[4]

Around the early 1970s, Bo Diddley moved to Florida, where he would spend the last years of his life. He lived in several places there, including Archer, Gainesville, and Hawthorne. He still toured occasionally and performed concerts, but his health was not as good as it had been. It became more and more exhausting to get on stage, play his music, and use the dance moves some people said inspired Elvis Presley.

In 2007, Diddley had a stroke. Some sources say the stroke ended his career because of how difficult talking and singing became. Other people say that Diddley didn't let that stop him, and that he continued recording, playing, and singing until he died at age 79 of heart failure on June 2, 2008.

THE ED SULLIVAN SHOW

Bo Diddley wasn't the only person to be banned from *The Ed Sullivan Show*. Sullivan was famous for introducing to the world small bands and artists who were on the rise. For many people, the first time they saw or heard Elvis Presley or the Beatles was on *Ed Sullivan*. Most musicians were very excited to be invited to the show. There were, however, quite a few people whom Sullivan banned from ever returning.

The Rolling Stones performed for Sullivan in 1964 and were then told they'd never perform there again. Why? Sullivan was angry at how much noise the largely teenage audience made. The ban was only temporary. The Rolling Stones appeared on the show a total of four times. On their fourth appearance, they were asked to change one of the lines to their song "Let's Spend the Night Together" to "let's spend some time together." Mick Jagger, the lead singer, did as he was told. However, he rolled his eyes at the audience each time he sang the edited line.[5]

In 1967, the Doors performed on *The Ed Sullivan Show*. At the last minute, the band was asked to change one of the lines in their hit song "Light My Fire." The lead singer, Jim Morrison, did not make the change and sang the song with the original lyrics. Sullivan banned the Doors from the show, canceling six already scheduled appearances.[6]

When the Beatles first performed on *The Ed Sullivan Show*, a record 73 million people tuned in.

Chapter Five
HONORING THE LEGEND

When Bo Diddley died in 2008, the people of Florida wanted to celebrate his life. In Archer, where he had lived for more than 20 years, a parade and festival were held in his honor. At his funeral in Gainesville, more than 500 people came. Celebrities Tom Petty, ZZ Top, and George Thorogood sent flowers. Friends, family, and bandmates of Diddley's got up and shared stories about the blues singer.[1] They talked about how generous he had become as he got older. "There was one thing he wouldn't give me. That's his hat," Diddley's brother, the Reverend Kenneth Haynes, said at the funeral.[2]

The mayor of Gainesville, Pegeen Hanrahan, also spoke. She mentioned one of Diddley's most famous songs about love. "When the question is asked, 'Who Do You Love?', it's you, Bo."[3] She also announced that the Gainesville town square would be renamed the Bo Diddley Community Plaza.

While Diddley was always quick to talk about his music, he was often slower to talk about his family. This didn't mean they were not important to him.

Diddley was known for inviting up-and-coming talents to perform with him. This includes the singer Marvin Gaye. When Diddley knew him, Gaye was Diddley's valet. Some say Gaye's vocals can be heard on the song "Who Do You Love?"

When he died, Diddley had 4 children, 15 grandchildren, 15 great-grandchildren, and 4 great-great-grandchildren. At his funeral, his Talent Source business manager, Faith Fusillo, told his family, "Please know this, because I know Bo Diddley. As much as you loved him, he loved you more."[4]

After the funeral, Gainesville held a concert to honor him. There, members of Diddley's family performed a few of his songs alongside some of the blues singers' old bandmates.

Bo Diddley Plaza in Gainesville, Florida

When the Bo Diddley Community Plaza was officially named in 2009, Diddley's grandson Garry Mitchell said this to Gainesville: "Gainesville's been really good to my granddad. The love that you've shown throughout his career . . . it meant a lot because it kept him here, and it kept a whole lot of us here. [Gainesville] may not be a major city on the map, but Bo Diddley left his star here."[5]

While Bo Diddley did not start receiving recognition for his work until late in life, the awards and acknowledgments came fast at the end of his life and in the years after his death. He belongs to the Blues

Another of Bo Diddley's guitars in the Rock and Roll Hall of Fame Museum.

Hall of Fame and the Rock and Roll Hall of Fame, as well as the Florida Artists and Mississippi Musicians Hall of Fame. In 1996, Diddley received a Lifetime Achievement Award from the Rhythm and Blues Foundation. In 1998, he received another Lifetime Achievement Award, this one from the National Academy of Recording Arts and Sciences.

The Bo Diddley Plaza in Gainesville is just one place of many that commemorates the famous musician. In the years since his death, Diddley's gravesite at Bronson Cemetery has become a popular tourist destination. The headstone is so large, it is almost the length of a car. It features an image of his trademark bright red square guitar. Across the top of the stone are the words, "The Mighty Bo Diddley: I'm a Man." A line across the bottom describes Diddley as a pioneer, an icon, a pharaoh, the originator, and legend. The headstone also calls him, "A Man Who Lived an Abundant Life and Left a Fruitful Legacy." Archer, Florida, is so proud of the Bo Diddley legacy, the town declared December 30th Bo Diddley Day.

When it comes to appreciating all the ways Diddley has contributed to the world of music, there are no bigger fans than other musicians.

Jo Satriani

American guitarist Joe Satriani said, "Bo Diddley gave us so much. He was an essential part of rock 'n' roll. It couldn't have happened without him." Bob Weir of the Grateful Dead has said, "When musicians get together and they're working up stuff, it's quite common to hear somebody say, 'I want you to play this Bo Diddley,' and everybody knows what that means." Australian singer-songwriter Keith Urban once opened for Bo Diddley in New York City. He made sure to stick around to watch Diddley's performance. Urban was glad he did, or he would have missed a really great compliment from someone who rarely gave them. "After his show, we were packing up backstage," said Urban. "And in walks Bo and he says, 'Hey, boy, was that you just pickin' on that there guitar?' I said, 'Yeah.' He said, 'Mmm, you're a good guitar player, boy,' and then he just nodded and walked away."[6]

Many musicians, artists, and bands have done covers of the Originator's songs. Diddley's tunes have been used in movies and TV shows, and he's been invited on late-night talk shows. Concerts have been held in his honor and articles have been published on how Diddley helped define R&B. His style can be heard in the music of Bruce Springsteen, the Rolling Stones, the Doors, and the Who. Most recently, the band the Blasters has been opening up about being influenced by Diddley as well. Just bend your ear to the music and listen for that history-making sound called the Diddley Beat.

And if other aspiring guitar players or blues singers want advice from Bo Diddley, they can follow the pep talk he gave himself about pursuing a musical career. "I kept pounding at it," he told reporter Richard Harrington. "It was like being in jail and you've got a chisel and a hammer and the chisel is dull, but you keep beating at that same spot and eventually you're going to get a hole through there. It might take a little while, but you keep pounding. And you might not get out but you can see through it, dig?"[7]

Bo Diddley was known to bring a smile to everyone he met. With his music legacy, fans are smiling still.

FEMALE BANDMATES

"I'm Looking for a Woman" isn't just the name of one of Bo Diddley's songs. In the era that Bo Diddley was playing his music, women were rarely in bands. Their names appeared in song titles and in lyrics, but they were rarely on stage themselves. This was not true when it came to Bo Diddley's bands. In his career, Diddley played alongside at least three female musicians.

In 1957, Diddley's guitarist Jody Williams left to join the military. Diddley replaced him with Peggy Jones. It is her guitar that can be heard in such famous tunes as Diddley's "Mona," "Say Man," "Hey, Bo Diddley," and "Bo Diddley's a Gunslinger." Besides the electric guitar, she also played the piano, and she sang. She played such an important role for Diddley, she became known as Lady Bo.

Diddley liked giving his female bandmates nicknames. After Lady Bo, Norma-Jean Wofford joined the band. Quickly nicknamed The Duchess, Wofford joined Diddley on his tour of England in 1962. She and Diddley were so close, Bo told everyone she was his sister. He said he did this so that other band members wouldn't approach her for dates.

The woman who spent the most time playing with Bo Diddley was Debby Hastings. She and her electric bass joined him around 1984 and she eventually became his music director. She stayed with Diddley until he died in 2008. At his funeral, she said, "He was the rock that the roll is built on."[8]

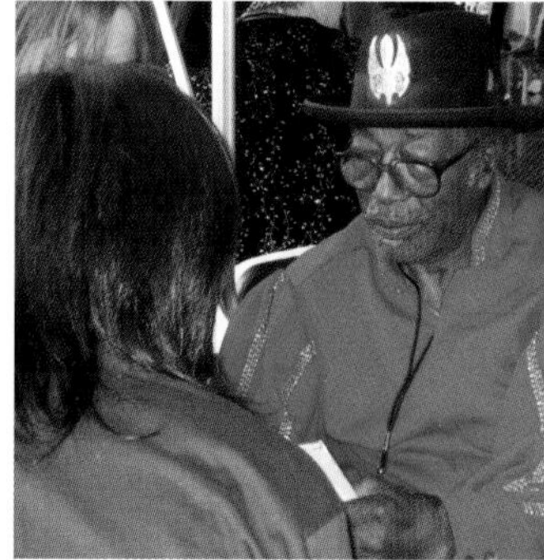

Bo Diddley was known to treat women with respect, even when just signing autographs.

CHRONOLOGY

1928 Bo Diddley is born on December 30 as Ellis or Elias Landry.

1936? Diddley is adopted by his mother's cousin, Gussie McDaniel.

1951 Diddley meets Billy Boy Arnold and Jody Williams.

1955 Diddley creates the Diddley Beat. Chess Records picks up Diddley's music. Diddley performs on *The Ed Sullivan Show.*

1971 Diddley moves to Los Lunas, New Mexico, and becomes a deputy sheriff.

1973 Diddley is in the music documentary *Let the Good Times Roll.*

1983 He plays a pawnbroker in the movie *Trading Places.*

1987 Diddley is inducted into the Rock and Roll Hall of Fame.

1989 He performs at the inauguration of George H. W. Bush.

1989 Diddley is in a Nike commercial.

1996 He receives a Lifetime Achievement Award from the Rhythm and Blues Foundation.

1998 He receives a Lifetime Achievement Award from the National Academy of Recording Arts and Sciences. He appears in the movie *Blues Brothers 2000.*

2003 Diddley performs with musician Tom Petty in Milwaukee, Wisconsin.

2007 A stroke makes it difficult for him to perform.

2008 Bo Diddley dies of heart failure on June 2.

2009 The Bo Diddley Community Plaza in Gainesville, Florida, is officially given its new name.

2015 Lady Bo (Peggy Jones) dies at the age of 75.

2017 A stretch of highway seven miles long in Mississippi is named the Bo Diddley Memorial Highway.

Chapter One: Becoming a Star

1. "Bo Diddley—Ed Sullivan Show 1955." *YouTube*. June 5 2017. https://www.youtube.com/watch?v=38G5MKn3jlw
2. *The Ed Sullivan Show*. "Bo Diddley on the Ed Sullivan Show Story." http://www.edsullivan.com/bo-diddley-on-the-ed-sullivan-show-story/
3. Ibid.
4. Havers, Richard. "Willie Dixon—The Greatest Blues Songwriter." U Discover Music. January 2017. https://www.udiscovermusic.com/stories/willie-dixon-the-greatest-blues-songwriter/

Chapter Two: From Violins to Square Guitars

1. Mississippi Blues Trail. "Bo Diddley." http://www.msbluestrail.org/blues-trail-markers/bo-diddley
2. *Rolling Stone*. "Bo Diddley Bio." https://www.rollingstone.com/music/artists/bo-diddley/biography
3. Harrington, Richard. "Fame Courts a New Bo." *Washington Post*. November 1, 1990. https://www.washingtonpost.com/archive/lifestyle/1990/11/01/fame-courts-a-new-bo/1a0c2159-b909-4d8b-8742-d7415530d9f8/?utm_term=.224b5eaea334
4. Dahl, Bill. "Featured Interview—Billy Boy Arnold." *Blues Blast Magazine*, November 2017. http://www.bluesblastmagazine.com/featured-interview-billy-boy-arnold/

Chapter Three: Discovering the Diddley Beat

1. Unterberger, Richie. "Billy Boy Arnold." Richie Unterberger, 2000–2010. http://www.richieunterberger.com/arnold.html
2. Ibid.
3. The History Engine. "Bo Diddley Records 'I'm a Man.' " https://historyengine.richmond.edu/episodes/view/5339

Chapter Four: From Cover to Covered

1. Eric Burdon & The Animals. "The Story of Bo Diddley." YouTube, published by Rootheart, July 26, 2009. https://www.youtube.com/watch?v=swPzNFxsghc

2. Hamlin, Bradley Mason. "Eric Burdon Interview." *Mystery Island Magazine*, September 2009. http://mysteryisland.net/ericburdon
3. "Grateful Dead Man Remembers Bo Diddley." *NME*, June 2, 2008. https://www.nme.com/news/music/bo-diddley-11-1333433
4. Ellis, Josh. "The Greatest Ad Campaign Ever?" *Success*, February 2014. https://www.success.com/article/the-greatest-ad-campaign-ever
5. Swanson, Dave. "Why the Rolling Stones Were Forced to 'Spend Some Time' with Ed Sullivan." Ultimate Classic Rock. http://ultimateclassicrock.com/rolling-stones-ed-sullivan-spend-some-time/
6. Whitaker, Sterling. "Why the Doors Got Banned from 'The Ed Sullivan Show.'" Ultimate Classic Rock. http://ultimateclassicrock.com/the-doors-banned-from-the-ed-sullivan-show-september-17-1967/

Chapter Five: Honoring the Legend

1. Hendrickson, Matt. "Friends, Admirers Honor Bo Diddley at Funeral in Gainesville." *Rolling Stone*, June 9, 2008. https://www.rollingstone.com/music/news/friends-admirers-honor-bo-diddley-at-funeral-in-gainesville-20080609
2. "Bo Diddley Funeral a Rocking Sendoff." *CBS News*, June 7, 2008. https://www.cbsnews.com/news/bo-diddley-funeral-a-rocking-sendoff/
3. Ibid.
4. Ibid.
5. Stuckey, Michelle. "Plaza Renamed in Honor of Legend Bo Diddley." *The Gainesville Sun*, June 6, 2009. http://www.gainesville.com/news/20090606/plaza-renamed-in-honor-of-legend-bo-diddley
6. Graff, Gary. "Remembering Bo Diddley." *Billboard*. May 2009. https://www.billboard.com/articles/news/268504/remembering-bo-diddley
7. Harrington, Richard. "Fame Courts a New Bo." *The Washington Post*, November 1, 1990. https://www.washingtonpost.com/archive/lifestyle/1990/11/01/fame-courts-a-new-bo/1a0c2159-b909-4d8b-8742-d7415530d9f8/?utm_term=.da3f98e3d9f6
8. Dean, Bill. "Beat Lives On at a Memorial for Bo Diddley." *The New York Times*, June 9, 2008. http://www.nytimes.com/2008/06/09/arts/music/09diddley.html

Books

Austen, Jake. *TV-a-Go-Go: Rock on TV from American Bandstand to American Idol.* Chicago: Chicago Review Press, 2005.

Christenson, Bonnie. *Elvis: The Story of the Rock and Roll King.* New York: Henry Holt and Co., 2015.

Dahl, Bill. *The Art of the Blues: A Visual Treasury of Black Music's Golden Age*. Chicago: University of Chicago Press, 2016.

Mahin, Michael. *Muddy: The Story of Blues Legend Muddy Waters.* New York: Atheneum Publishing, 2017.

O'Connor, Jim, and Who HQ. *What Is Rock and Roll?* (What Was?) London, England: Penguin Workshop Press, 2017.

Roza, Greg. *Bo Diddley: Rock & Roll All-Star.* New York: Gareth Stevens Publishing, 2010.

Works Consulted

"Bo Diddley." *Telegraph*, June 2, 2008. http://www.telegraph.co.uk/news/obituaries/2066171/Bo-Diddley.html

"Bo Diddley on *The Ed Sullivan Show*." *CC Rider*, November, 2015. http://ccriderblues.com/bo-diddley-on-the-ed-sullivan-show/

Dean, Bill. "Beat Lives On at a Memorial for Bo Diddley." *New York Times*, June 9, 2008. http://www.nytimes.com/2008/06/09/arts/music/09diddley.html

"Gone but Not Forgotten: Bo Diddley." *Blues and Music News*, March 4, 2015. http://bg.buddyguy.com/gone-but-not-forgotten-bo-diddley/

Hamlin, Bradley Mason. "Eric Burdon Interview." *Mystery Island Magazine*, September 2009. http://mysteryisland.net/ericburdon

Nash, J. D. "21 Things You Didn't Know About Bo Diddley (And One You Didn't Know About Marvin Gaye." *American Blues Scene*, November 2015. https://www.americanbluesscene.com/facts-about-bo-diddley-beat/

Ratliff, Ben. "Bo Diddley, Who Gave Rock His Beat, Dies at 79." *New York Times*, June 3, 2008. http://www.nytimes.com/2008/06/03/arts/music/03diddley.html

On the Internet

Bo Diddley
http://www.bodiddley.com/

Rock & Roll Hall of Fame: Bo Diddley
https://www.rockhall.com/inductees/bo-diddley

amateur (AM-ih-chur)—A person who does an activity for fun and not for profit.

blues (BLOOZ)— form of music originated by African Americans in the Deep South of the U.S. around the end of the 19th century

campaign (kam-PAYN)—A series of advertisements that promote one particular product.

civil rights (SIH-vul RYTS)—The battle for racial equality in the law.

documentary (dok-yoo-MEN-tuh-ree)—A film that examines or reports on factual events.

hand jive—A dance from the 1940s that involves tricky hand movements and clapping hands, wrists, and thighs to create a beat.

Juba dance—A traditionally African American dance that creates rhythm using the body by stomping; slapping one's thighs, chest, and face; and clapping.

originator (or-IH-jih-nay-tor)—The one who starts a movement or trend.

percussion (per-KUH-shun)—The striking of a musical instrument.

pharaoh (FAYR-oh)—Any of the kings of ancient Egypt.

segregate (SEH-greh-gayt)—To separate based on race.

stroke (STROHK)—An event in the brain in which blood vessels are either blocked or burst, causing brain damage and sometimes death.

trademark (TRAYD-mark)—A recognizable symbol, image, or action pertaining to something or someone.

washboard (WASH-bord)—A metal or wooden board with ridges used for scrubbing clothes and sometimes for making music.

PHOTO CREDITS: Cover—Bunkey's Pickle; p. 1—Masao Nakagami; p. 5—Mary; pp. 7, 22, 23, 29, 33—Public Domain; p . 7—Mark Feeney; p. 8—Peabody Awards, Don Hinchcliffe; p. 9—Mallory 1180; pp. 11, 37—Sam Howzit; p, 11—Uwe Dedering; p. 12—Runner1928; pp. 13, 19—Masashiro Sumori; p. 14—IMLS Digital Collections and Content; p. 15—Russell Lee, LOC; p. 16—John Lopez; p. 17—Beraldoleal; p. 20—Urko Dorronsoro; p. 21—John Harwood; p. 25—Rob Russell; p. 26—Jim Pietryga; p. 27—Heinrich Klaffs; p. 28—Dark Dwarf; pp. 30, 32, 35, 38, 40—Aconagua; p. 31—USNavy; p. 36—Todd van Hoosear; p. 38—Shape Prior.